This book belongs to

Millbrook Press
A division of Lerner Publishing Group, Inc.
241 First Avenue North
Minneapolis, MN 55401 USA

For reading levels and more information, look up this title at www.lernerbooks.com.

Designed by Danielle Carnito.
Main body text set in Imperfect OT 18/24.
Typeface provided by T26.
The illustrations in this book were created with watercolor and some digital wizardry.

Library of Congress Cataloging-in-Publication Data

Names: Levine, Sara (Veterinarian), author. | D'yans, Masha, illustrator.
Title: Flower talk : how plants use color to communicate / Sara Levine ; illustrations by Masha D'yans.
Description: Minneapolis : Millbrook Press, [2019] | Includes bibliographical references.
Identifiers: LCCN 2018012310 (print) | LCCN 2018008683 (ebook) | ISBN 9781541543782 (eb pdf) | ISBN 9781541519282 (lb : alk. paper)
Subjects: LCSH: Animal-plant relationships—Juvenile literature. | Flowers—Color—Juvenile literature. | Wildlife attracting—Juvenile literature.
Classification: LCC QH549.5 (print) | LCC QH549.5 .L48 2019 (ebook) | DDC 579/.178—dc23

LC record available at https://lccn.loc.gov/2018012310

Manufactured in the United States of America
1-44298-34558-8/2/2018

FLOWER TALK

HOW PLANTS USE COLOR TO COMMUNICATE

SARA LEVINE

ILLUSTRATIONS BY MASHA D'YANS

M Millbrook Press • Minneapolis

For Caedmon
—S.L.

To Colin, who
smells the
flowers with
me every day
—M.D.

HEY, YOU!

PSSST!

DOWN HERE!

THAT'S RIGHT—I'M A PLANT, AND I'M TALKING TO YOU!

But don't get too used to it. We don't make a habit of talking to humans.

I want to clear up some of your crazy ideas about what the colors of our flowers mean. We sit here growing, minding our own business while you guys go on about how red roses stand for love and white ones are good for weddings and all kinds of mushy, ridiculous stuff. What a load of fertilizer!

We're not using flowers to send information to you, so bud out, okay? We use our flowers to talk to the animals.

Why? We need some help down here. What would *you* do if your legs were stuck in the ground for your entire life?

HOW WOULD YOU EAT?

HOW WOULD YOU DRINK?

HOW WOULD YOU GET
YOUR PAJAMAS ON?

We can take care of *some* things ourselves. We get our food with help from the sun. And when it rains, our roots slurp up water.

But we need help making our seeds, *our babies*. What's more important than that? Without seeds, there'd be no more plants.

WE'D BE FINISHED.

KAPUT!

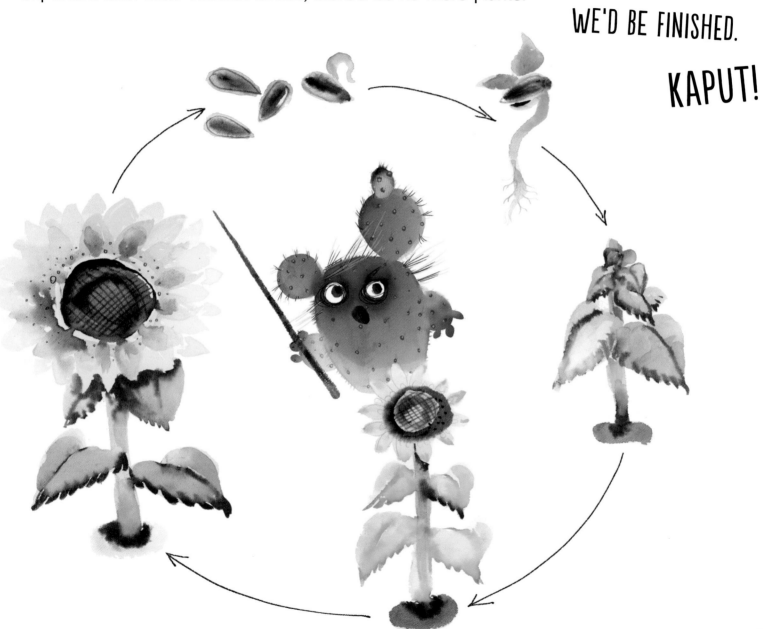

To make a seed, we need pollen from a *different plant* of our same type. How do we get that? We can't just waltz over and take some.

THAT'S WHY WE NEED ANIMALS.

Here's what we do: We trick them into carrying it for us. We're nice about it, though—we pay them a little something for their efforts.

Well . . . usually.

How do we get them to help?

We advertise. We hold up big signs. Our flowers are the signs. They say,

Come on over. We have a special treat for you.

And believe me, they come. Who wouldn't?—especially if they're hungry! If we're in luck, they bring along some pollen from a flower they visited earlier. Do they know they're doing this? Who knows?

And who cares! It works, and everyone's happy.

SO WHAT'S THE DEAL WITH THE COLORS?

A flower's color invites specific animals to visit. You seem like a bright kid, so I'm going to let you in on the conversation. Then maybe you could do me a favor and tell the other humans about it, okay?

RED FLOWERS ARE USUALLY TALKING TO BIRDS.

The red flower's message is a top secret one, for birds only. Most other pollinators are insects, and they can't see the color red.

A red flower says: "Hey, hummingbird—over here! Carry my pollen, and I'll give you a sip of nectar."

By the way, red flowers don't have much of an odor. Birds have a horrible sense of smell, so why bother making perfume for them?

BLUE AND PURPLE FLOWERS TALK TO BEES.

Bees need flower pollen to feed their babies. They have special pockets on their legs to carry it home to their young. But some pollen always gets stuck on their bodies and passed to the next flowers they visit.

Blue and purple flowers are saying: "Yo, bee! Could you help me move some of this pollen? And take some home for the kids!" See? We can be thoughtful too.

YELLOW FLOWERS ARE ALSO TALKING TO BEES.

Bees are our top helpers. I heard that scientists just figured out that bees have three favorite colors: blue, purple, and yellow. Took you guys long enough! We've known this for ages. That's why so many of us make flowers in these colors. We like the reliable help.

Here's what a yellow flower says: "Bees, bargain basement this way—free food!"

SOME WHITE FLOWERS TALK TO MOTHS AND BATS.

Moths and bats fly mostly at night. And when it's dark outside, what color shows up best? White, of course!

White flowers are like giant signs that say, "Hey, come get your free nectar here." White flowers also put out perfume as an extra guide to help these animals find them. Frankly, I don't care for it, myself, but I guess to a moth or a bat, it smells pretty good.

BROWN FLOWERS OFTEN TALK TO FLIES.

Here's what they're saying: "Get a whiff of our perfume. It's stinky, just the way you like it."

This is true. Brown flowers reek like something dead and rotten. And flies need to lay their eggs on dead things so their maggot babies will have something to eat when they hatch. (I know—so gross!)

But a brown flower doesn't help a mama fly at all. She gets drawn in by the stench, but there's no meat there—just a flower tricking a bug into doing work for free. The flower gets pollen, but the fly gets nothing. The only rotten thing around here is the deal.

GREEN FLOWERS AREN'T TALKING TO ANYONE.

Are they just shy? No. They don't talk to animals because they don't need help. Their pollen is carried by the wind. Plants with green flowers are just green all over because they don't need animals to notice them. Would you bother getting dressed up if you didn't need to? I know I wouldn't.

DO ANIMALS ONLY GO TO FLOWERS THAT ARE THEIR FAVORITE COLORS?

No. But usually they do.

For example, butterflies are drawn more to a flower's shape than its color. Butterflies like a steady platform to land on and tubes filled with nectar to sip with their long, curly tongues. They visit flowers of many colors. But even butterflies have favorites: white, purple, yellow, pink, red, and orange.

That's a lot of favorites, don't you think?

It's been good chatting, but it's time for you to leave now. Go take a hike.
I'm pretty busy, in case you haven't noticed. I'm making a new flower. It's going
to be yellow with a nice, roomy platform. I'm just about done with it.

BUT BEFORE YOU LEAVE, DO YOU WANT TO GUESS WHO I'M GETTING READY TO TALK TO NEXT?

MORE ABOUT POLLINATION

Pollination is the way plants make new seeds. Here's how it works:

PARTS OF A FLOWER

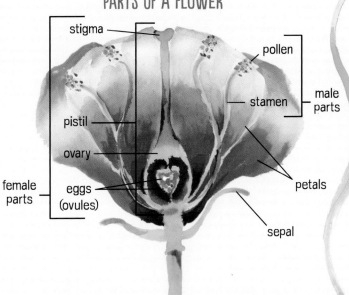

stigma

pollen

pistil

stamen — male parts

ovary

female parts

eggs (ovules)

petals

sepal

To make a seed, a plant needs to combine pollen with an egg. Sometimes the pollen and the egg can be from the same plant (which is called self-pollination). Usually they come from different plants of the same species (which is called cross-pollination).

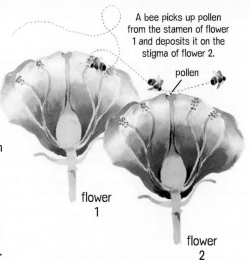

A bee picks up pollen from the stamen of flower 1 and deposits it on the stigma of flower 2.

pollen

flower 1

flower 2

STEP 1

How does the pollen get to the eggs? In some types of plants, wind carries the pollen. For many other plants, an animal pollinator helps out. The animal carries the pollen from a stamen, the male part of a flower, to a pistil, the female part of a flower. The pistil holds the eggs inside.

STEP 2

For pollination to work, the pollen needs to land on just the right spot—the stigma, which is the sticky top of the pistil. When the pollen lands perfectly, a tube grows up from the eggs, making a sort of slide for the pollen to travel down to meet the eggs (also called ovules).

Now the pollen joins with the eggs to make seeds. The male parts of the flower, the stamen, aren't needed anymore, so they fall off. The petals aren't needed anymore to attract the insects, so they fall off too.

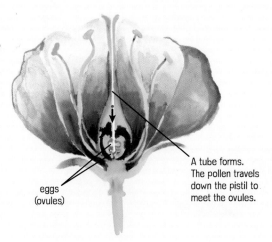

eggs (ovules)

A tube forms. The pollen travels down the pistil to meet the ovules.

STEP 3

The ovary grows bigger and bigger around the seeds. The ovary becomes the fruit with the seeds inside, ready to someday grow into a new plant. It could be an apple, a pumpkin, peas in their pod, peanuts in their shell, or many others. Some of these aren't commonly called fruits, but they are. If a food has seeds in it, it is botanically a fruit!

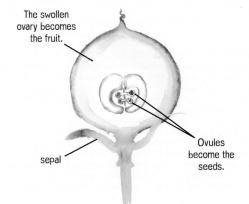

The swollen ovary becomes the fruit.

sepal

Ovules become the seeds.

PROTECTING OUR POLLINATORS

Did you know that some insect pollinators are in trouble? This is a big problem because plants rely on these animals to carry pollen. Without pollination, plants can't make new seeds. And without seeds, new plants can't grow.

Many people don't think about how important plants are. We actually need them to survive. Plants are our food and our shelter, and they even make the air we breathe.

Here are some things you and your family can do to help support the pollinators:

1. Don't use chemicals that hurt insects on your lawn or garden.
2. Plant a bee or butterfly garden so these animal pollinators have a new place to eat and live.
3. Tell other people about this problem so they can help too.

For more tips, check out Pollinator Partnership at http://pollinator.org.

READ MORE ABOUT PLANTS AND POLLINATORS

Anthony, Joseph. *In a Nutshell*. Nevada City, CA: Dawn Publications, 1999.

Barton, Bethany. *Give Bees a Chance*. New York: Viking, 2017.

Brenner, Barbara. *One Small Place in a Tree*. New York: HarperCollins, 2004.

Brown, Ruth. *Ten Seeds*. New York: Knopf, 2010.

Chin, Jason. *Redwoods*. New York: Flashpoint, 2009.

Griffin Burns, Loree. *The Hive Detectives: Chronicle of a Honey Bee Catastrophe*. Boston: Houghton Mifflin Books for Children, 2010.

Hirsch, Rebecca. *Plants Can't Sit Still*. Minneapolis: Millbrook Press, 2016.

Stewart, Melissa. *A Seed Is the Start*. Washington, DC: National Geographic, 2018.